I need you to help me with this book.

When I say

BOO

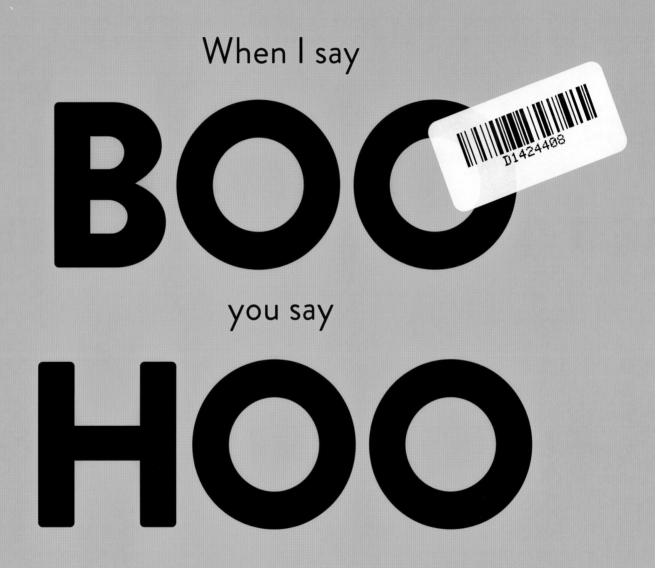

you say

HOO

Can you do that?
Great, let's practise.

BOO
BOO
BOO

Hang on, you don't have to

CRY

Now, if you see a

TREE

you shout

YES,

YOU!

There's no one else here.

OK! OK! OK!
This book isn't all about you.

Here's another thing. If you see the colour

BLUE

shout

STINKY POO

WHAT

did you just

SAY?

OH

NO!

I thought that's what you said.
*Can you **not** say that? It's* **RUDE**.

You're embarrassing me in front of my friend.

This is

BOO

Sorry, I'll speak up. This is

BOO

Are you even listening to me? It's

BOO

NO!

NO!

NO!

NOT
STINKY POO

It's **BOO**, the ghost.
And **BOO** is afraid of the dark.

So, if it goes

DARK

I need you to

BARK like this WOOF! WOOF! WOOF!

AAHHH!

Who turned off the lights?

BOO

is scared.

WHAT? WHERE? WHO?

Look, now you've embarrassed

BOO

You're barking again!

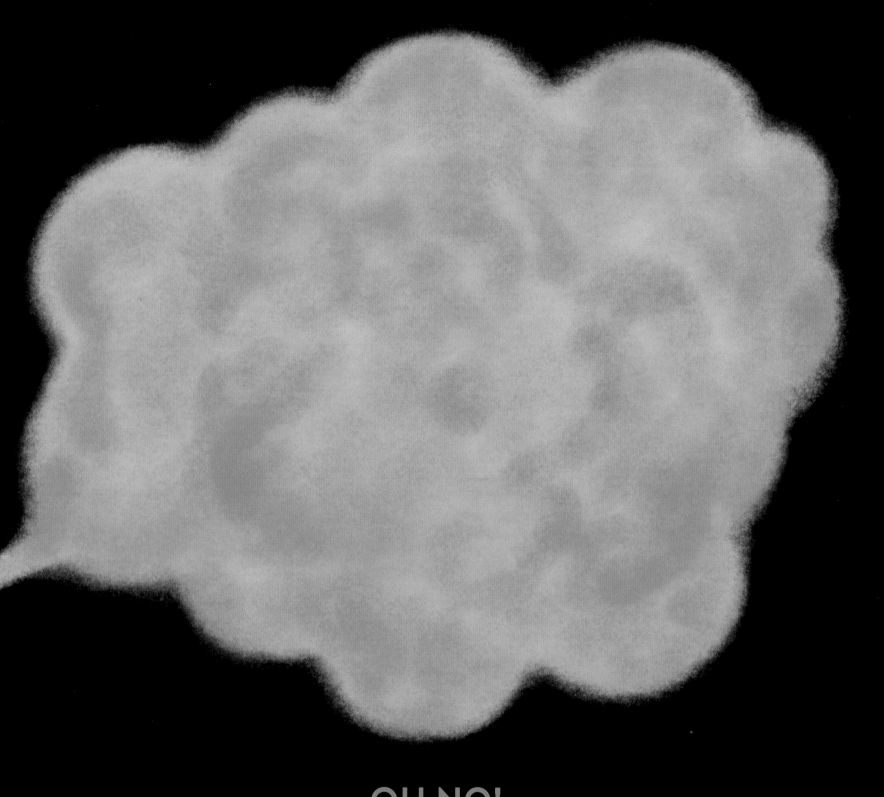

OH NO!
Look what you've made **BOO** do!

That's not nice.

BOO

has run away to hide.

But what's he hiding behind?

BEHIND YOU?

You really think
there's a ghost behind you?

Right, one last thing to remember.

If you see

CROWS

hold your

NOSE

What's wrong?

Can you smell something?

A STINKY
POO?

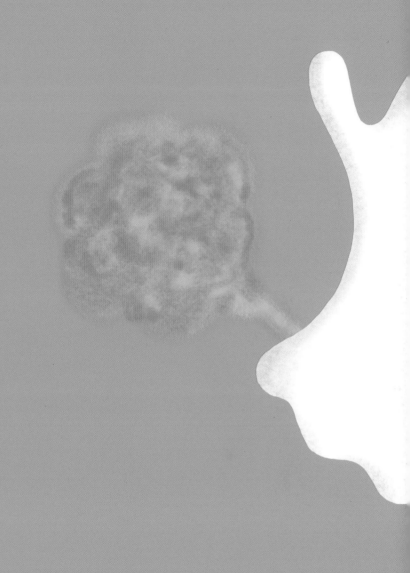

Here we go again.

Who did it?

YOU DID A

STIN
PO

KYO?

ARE
YOU
SURE?

OK, now I'm confused. Was it

YOU

was it

BOO

or are you barking like a dog
so you can blame a dog
that isn't even in this book?

Please just tell me who it was.

PHEW!

So that's what the smell is.

Well, in the end it's always
good to tell the truth.

Just ask

BOO

BOO

needs to go home
before it gets dark.

Say bye-bye

BOO

Now, who wants
to read this book again?